The Eleventh Commandment:
Domestic Violence Through the Eyes of God

Printed in the United States of America
©2007 by Rhonda Skinner Sullivan
Publisher: We Family Ministries
      P.O. Box 40644
      Jacksonville, FL 32203

Library of Congress Cataloging pending
ISBN: 0-9788545-4-3

No part of this book may be reproduced or transmitted in any form or by any means, electronic or mechanical, including photocopying, recording, or by any information retrieval system, without permission in writing from the author or publisher.

DEDICATION

This book is dedicated to all of the people who have broken the bondage of domestic violence over their lives. We are more than conquerors through Christ Jesus.

To my abuser, thank you for propelling me into the place of abundant growth and blessings that God had for me.

For all of you who are still living with an abusive spouse, my hope is that this book will empower you by helping you to see how very much God loves you, wants you to have life, and to have it more abundantly.
Jesus is the answer!

FOREWORD

The Spirit of the Sovereign Lord is on me, because the Lord has anointed me to preach good news to the poor. He has sent me to bind up the broken hearted, to proclaim freedom for the captives and release from darkness for the prisoners, to proclaim the year of the Lord's favor and the day of vengeance of our God, to comfort all who mourn, and provide for those who grieve in Zion to bestow on them a crown of beauty instead of ashes, the oil of gladness instead of mourning, and a garment of praise instead of a spirit of despair. They will be called oaks of righteousness, a planting of the Lord for the display of his splendor. (Isaiah 61:1-3)

On October 17, 2005, God gave me a revelation; "Free to Serve, Free to Love, Free to Live!" At that time I had no idea what that revelation meant. I searched the scriptures for the meaning and even hurried to find a tangible interpretation of the vision that accompanied it. The hurried search proved unsuccessful at that time. See, what you don't know about me is that I am a survivor. I overcame an abusive spouse, the hurt of numerous attempts at reconciliation, and the trauma of divorce. Later, through my desire to find spiritual peace, the meaning of that revelation was revealed to me. This book is the fruit of that search. Psalms 119:24 says, "Thy testimonies are my delight and my counselors." My hope is that my experience as the Christian wife of an abusive husband will serve as a testimony for others who struggle to find Godly answers while standing through the trial of an ungodly situation.

As a believer in an abusive relationship, I struggled with many things. My main desire was to stay in God's will by being obedient to His Word. I searched the scriptures daily for words of encouragement, justification, and guidance. I prayed daily for revelation and insight into why

TABLE OF CONTENTS

6	A Day In The Life
8	He Says, She Says...
15	Anointed Covenant?
19	Submission or Abuse
21	Up Front and Personal
27	Salt Of The Earth
32	Invisible Tears
39	Heavenly Counselor
42	What To Do Until You Get Through
45	A Father's Love
49	God's Will Not Ours
53	When Enough Is Too Much
59	Refining The Salt
62	No Pearls For Pigs
64	Soup For Your Soul
67	Sinless
69	Highly Esteemed
71	Pouring Out Poison
74	The Power of Prayer
75	Restoration Proclamation
78	Spiritual Swap-meet
81	Fasting Creed
82	Victory In Jesus
84	Help For The Helpmate
85	Healing The Hurt

bad things happen to good people. At one point, I was even mad at God for allowing the abuse to happen to me. As I progressed to a point where the abuse had become life-threatening, I was forced to leave and ultimately file for a divorce. Even after filing for the divorce I dealt with condemnation and regret; often feeling like I had failed as a person, as a wife, as a mother, and more importantly as a believer.

That constant feeling of failure forced me to search deeper into God's word for answers. Much of what you will read is the result of that search. This book is a compilation of the many things that God revealed to me during my trial and subsequently my healing process. It was written for the purpose of lighting your path to deliverance. I believe that by sharing what I have learned, you too can be healed. Just as God delivered David from King Saul's hurtful sword, you too can be delivered. As you read, remember to seek God for revelation as it pertains to your individual situation. Allow the Holy Spirit to guide you as your broken heart is mended. You can be given liberty over your captor and your prison door can be opened. God will free you to live the abundant life that He has for you. Be still and know that he is God!

A DAY IN THE LIFE

"One Believer's Journey"

This is a story about a beautiful princess. She was an ordinary person with extraordinary potential. She was like many other women in that she desired to fall in love, get married, and live happily ever after. One day, she meets a handsome prince and after a long courtship, they are married. Little did she know that her prince would turn into a frog. Here is a sneak peek into the life of that princess and how she ultimately found the desires of her heart.

I am that princess. I am a believer and here is my journey from abuse to restoration. The abuse started before I married my husband. First came the subtle hints of jealously, followed by name calling, accusations, and maliciousness. About six months into our relationship the physical abuse started. The first time was the worst, probably because I was so surprised to find myself in a situation like that. It wasn't supposed to happen to me! During that incident, I was repeatedly punched in the face
and body leaving me with a bruised brain, a bloody nose, two black eyes, and multiple bruises to my body. Little did I know that this was the first of many abusive episodes. Despite the abuse, we were married a year later. My hope was that marriage would help my prince to feel loved and that the abuse would stop.

Wrong! The abuse continued. The prince simply became craftier. He realized that punching me in the face could get him arrested. So, choking me became his method of choice. To ensure that he kept his control over me, he maintained a continuous flow of threats against my life. Since I am writing this book, I guess you figured out that he never quite succeeded in murdering me, not physically
anyway.

The prince (a frog by now) was not just abusive toward me

but toward himself as well. He was a drug addict, a chain smoker, and a sex addict who enjoyed masturbation and pornography. His other hobbies included standing on the corner with drug dealers and drug addicts, lying, stealing, and adultery. He ultimately ended up in a place of depression, where his days consisted of sleeping all day and maintaining a sexually impure life at night. He could not keep a job, experienced severe financial difficulty, and ultimately lost everything that he knew to be good. He lost his family, his home, and himself.

So, you might ask, "What happened to the beautiful princess?" She was saved by a mighty King. She was blessed with many gifts; the greatest of them, salvation. She was adopted into a loving church family. She found her prince charming, a mighty man of God, and she and her daughter are living happily every after.

Now, if only my journey was that simple. As the rest of the story unfolds keep in mind that this is not just my story. It is the story of millions of other believers. My guess is that if you are reading this book, then you may be one character or another in a fairy tale like mine. Let my story be proof to you that this King, our Lord and Savior Jesus Christ, has many gifts waiting for you. You only need to claim them. There is no charge. The debt has already been paid!

HE SAYS, SHE SAYS...BUT WHAT DOES GOD SAY?

> I have told you these things, so that in me you may have peace. In this world you will have trouble. But take heart! I have overcome the world.
> (John 16:33)

"He says, she says..."

Webster's 1828 Dictionary describes abuse as the following:

- To use with bad motives or to wrong purposes; as, to abuse rights or privileges.
- To violate; to defile by improper sexual intercourse.
- To deceive; to impose on.
- To treat rudely, or with reproachful language; to revile.
- To pervert the meaning of; to misapply; as to abuse words.
- Improper treatment or employment; application to a wrong purpose; as an abuse of our natural powers; an abuse of civil rights, or of religious privileges; abuse of advantages

The National Center for Victims of Crime describes domestic violence as the willful intimidation, assault, battery, sexual assault, or other abusive behavior perpetrated by one family member, household member, or intimate partner against another.

Webster, Noah. Noah Webster's 1828 American Dictionary of the English Language. 1828

Domestic violence is about power and control. The abuser may use many different techniques to manipulate the victim. Let's look at each one and gain biblical insight into what God's word says about them.

Physical abuse - any action that causes physical harm to the victim
- hitting
- pushing
- kicking

Threats/Coercion - making or carrying out threats to harm the victim
- stalking
- jealousy
- falsely accusing the victim of infidelity or disloyalty

Intimidation - using facial gestures and actions to instill fear in the victim
- yelling
- angry looks

Emotional Abuse - demeaning the victim verbally or indirectly
- name calling
- putting down the victim

Isolation - keeping the victim away from anyone who could influence them
- controlling who the victim communicates with
- keeping the victim from spending time with family and friends
- putting down the victim's friends
- moving frequently
- restricting access to transportation
- keeping the victim busy with "chores" or "duties" to limit personal time

Minimizing, blaming, denying - down-playing the abuse

Using Children - manipulation of the victim by using the children to instill guilt or encourage compliance with the abuse

Economic Abuse - controlling the finances to encourage compliance with the abuse
- withholding money
- preventing the victim from having a job

Male Privilege - applies to situations where the victim is a woman
- treating the victim like she is inferior

All or most of these actions can exist in an abusive situation. For the purpose of this book, domestic violence and abuse will be used interchangeably. All scripture will be taken from the New International Version translation unless otherwise noted.

In 1 Samuel the relationship between David and King Saul is described. This book shows you that domestic abuse existed long before it had a name. Let's look at how this story fits the domestic violence mold.

In 1 Samuel, David after slaying Goliath went to live with King Saul in his home. Thereafter, King Saul isolated David by keeping him from returning to Bethlehem where his family lived. He blamed David for the people's admiration. Saul felt that somehow David had coerced the people into having respect and admiration for him. Saul used this as a reason to hate David and would ultimately
try to kill him. He frequently called David names to demean him. Saul attempted to control David's financial status by demoting him to captain without cause. Saul physically abused David and Jonathan (Saul's son) by repeatedly

throwing his javelin at them in anger. The bible is clear that Saul's intent was to kill them. Saul attempts to intimidate Jonathan and Michal, his children, to force them to help him betray David. This manipulation of Jonathan and Michal was used on numerous occasions to stalk and control David. Saul uses male privilege in his attempts to get Michal to betray David, her husband. So you can clearly see that Saul exhibited all of the characteristics of an abuser and David responded by acting in the role of a victim.

"God says..."

God's word gives us clear instruction on His stance on domestic violence. Domestic violence or any type of abuse is unacceptable in the eyes of God. As we search these scriptures, see if you can identify the characteristics of an abusive person. Malachi 2:16 demonstrates how God dislikes violence just as much as the act of divorce. He says, "I hate divorce...and I hate a man's covering himself with violence as well as with his garment". Ephesians 4:31 warns us of the need to get rid of all bitterness, rage, anger, brawling and slander, along with every form of malice. Galatians 5:19 tells us to avoid acts of a sinful nature. They are described as sexual immorality, impurity and debauchery, idolatry and witchcraft; hatred, discord, jealousy, fits of rage, selfish ambition, dissensions, factions and envy; drunkenness, orgies, and the like. In 2 Timothy 3:2-5, the Lord instructs us to have nothing to do with people who are lovers of themselves, lovers of money, boastful, proud, abusive, disobedient to their parents, ungrateful, unholy, without love, unforgiving, slanderous, without self control, brutal, not lovers of the good, treacherous, rash, conceited, lovers of pleasure rather than lovers of God... Some or all of these feelings of pride, superiority, and ungodliness are present in an abusive situation. They often serve as a catalyst for the perpetrator's abuse.

God's word gives us clear instruction on His stance on domestic violence. Domestic violence or any type of abuse is unacceptable in the eyes of God. As we search these scriptures, see if you can identify the characteristics of an abusive person. Malachi 2:16 demonstrates how God dislikes violence just as much as the act of divorce. He says, "I hate divorce...and I hate a man's covering himself with violence as well as with his garment". Ephesians 4:31 warns us of the need to get rid of all bitterness, rage, anger, brawling and slander, along with every form of malice. Galatians 5:19 tells us to avoid acts of a sinful nature. They are described as sexual immorality, impurity and debauchery, idolatry and witchcraft; hatred, discord, jealousy, fits of rage, selfish ambition, dissensions, factions and envy; drunkenness, orgies, and the like. In 2 Timothy 3:2-5, the Lord instructs us to have nothing to do with people who are lovers of themselves, lovers of money, boastful, proud, abusive, disobedient to their parents, ungrateful, unholy, without love, unforgiving, slanderous, without self control, brutal, not lovers of the good, treacherous, rash, conceited, lovers of pleasure rather than lovers of God... Some or all of these feelings of pride, superiority, and ungodliness are present in an abusive situation. They often serve as a catalyst for the perpetrator's abuse.

Seek His Face

Malachi 2:13-16
Another thing you do: You flood the Lord's alter with tears. You weep and wail because He no longer pays attention to your offerings or accepts them with pleasure from your hands. You ask, "Why? It is because the Lord is acting as witness between you and the wife of your youth, because you have broken faith with her, though she is your partner, the wife of your marriage covenant. Has not the Lord made them one? In flesh and spirit they are his. And why one? Because he was seeking godly offspring. So guard yourself in the spirit, and do not break faith with the wife of your youth. I hate divorce, says the Lord God of Israel, "and I hate a man's covering himself with violence as well as with his garment, "says the Lord Almighty. So guard yourself in the spirit and do not break faith with the wife of your youth.

1 Peter 3:7
Husbands, in the same way be considerate as you live with your wives, and treat them with respect as the weaker partner and as heirs with you of the gracious gift of life, so that nothing will hinder you prayers.

2 Timothy 3:2-5
People will be lovers of themselves, lovers of money, boastful, proud, abusive, disobedient to their parents, ungrateful, unholy, without love, unforgiving, slanderous, without self-control, brutal, not lovers of the good, treacherous, rash, conceited, lovers of pleasure rather than lovers of God-having a form of godliness but denying his power. Have nothing to do with them.

Galatians 5:19
The acts of the sinful nature are obvious: sexual immortality, impurity and debauchery; idolatry and witchcraft; hatred, discord, jealousy, fits of rage, selfish, ambition, dissensions, factions and envy, drunkenness, orgies, and the like. I warn you, as I did before, that those who live like this will not inherit the kingdom of God.

Proverbs 30:21-23
Under three things the earth trembles, under four it cannot bear up: a servant who becomes king, a fool who is full of food, an unloved woman who is married, and a maidservant who displaces her mistress.

Search Yourself
Is my spouse displaying any of the abuse behaviors listed above? If so, name them.

_____
_____
_____
_____
_____
_____
_____
_____
_____
_____
_____
_____
_____
_____
_____

ANNOINTED COVENANT OR AGGRAVATING INCONVENIENCE?

> Do not be unequally yoked with unbelievers. For what do righteousness and wickedness have in common? Or what fellowship can light have with darkness?
> (2 Corinthians 6:14)

"United by God..."

Marriage is one of the first institutions that God established between a man and a woman. Both men and women were created in his image as equal partners but they have distinctly different roles. The bible tells us that a husband is to be the head, or authority of his household. In performing his duty as head of his household, he should submit to God for direction. This role further challenges him with the responsibility of earning the respect of this family through living by Godly principles. As for the wife, she is to seek the Lord for direction in every area of life. Additionally, she is to submit to her husband out of love and respect for the Lord.

Mark 10:9 says, therefore what God has joined together, let no man separate. But how do you know if God put you and your spouse together? First, consider whether you are equally yoked as described in 2 Corinthians 6:14. Does your mate live under submission to the instructions in the rule book; the Holy Bible. Simply stated, is he/she obedient to God's word? Second, ask yourself if the fruits of the spirit are operating in your marriage? These fruits of the spirit are love, joy, peace, longsuffering, gentleness, goodness, faith, meekness, and temperance. This will be evidenced by obedience to the Word of God both publicly and privately. To have a successful marriage both husband and wife must read, understand, and obey the instructions. The Word of God has all of the requirements laid out for fruit. A good tree will bring forth good fruit; but a corrupt tree will bring forth evil fruit. In the same way, a good spouse will bring forth good fruit, the fruits of the Spirit.

Understanding God's expectations with regard to the marriage covenant is the key. The book of Ephesians explains this covenant in detail. A marital union, anointed by God, exemplifies the following promises:

Both husband and wife will:
1. Always give thanks for all things unto God and the Father in the name of our Lord Jesus Christ

2. Submit themselves one to another in the fear of God

Husbands will:
1. Leave his father and mother, and be joined with his wife, and the two will become one flesh

2. Be the head of his wife, even as Christ is the head of the church,: and he is savior of the body

3. Love his wife, even as Christ loved the church, and gave himself for it.

4. Love his wife as his own body

5. Love his wife even as himself

Wives will:
1. Submit herself unto her own husband, as unto the Lord

2. Be to her own husband in everything

3. Be subject unto Christ, as is the church

4. Reverence her husband

"Or Not..."

Avoid the pitfall of marrying Mr./Mrs. Wrong and hoping for them to change. If you are dating, considering marriage, or already married, pray for insight and revelation about every aspect of your relationship. If your mate is exhibiting some of these ungodly actions, don't give up just yet. This does not mean that you should continue to permit the sin. It simply means that you must look at your mate as a whole being, imperfect at times, as we all are. You should look at this as an opportunity to pray for him/her. Additionally, look for a willingness of your spouse to submit to God and a willingness to allow God to change him/her. If your mate is willing, trust me, GOD IS ABLE! He is faithful! Just as an earthly father wants only the best for his children, you must know that God would not chose anything less for you. God is not a man that he would lie. You must know that his word is true yesterday, today, and forever. God has a special mate for you who will love you the way Christ loved the church. Don't settle for less!

If you are already married and things in your marriage at not lining up with the word of God, pray for guidance as you assess your individual situation. Start with yourself. Recognize that any trial that you go through is really about YOU. Believe me, it will seem like the abuser is the one who needs a radical change. But keep in mind that God has a reason for the trial. You may find yourself being transformed. Every trial has a purpose. The ultimate purpose is for God's glory. Make sure that you are living a prayerful life of obedience. If you identify any shortcomings on your part, repent and pray for God's help to change. If you are unable to identify any areas of change for your life, praise God! Turn your prayer focus towards your spouse. God knows, your abuser needs it. Abusers are being strangled by the grasp of the enemy and if the abuse does not stop, God's wrath will be upon them, as well. You, the believer are called to intercede for your spouse and any other sinner. You may be his/her only hope.

Seek His Face

Ephesians 5:20-28, 31
Submit to one another out of reverence for Christ. Wives, submit to your husbands as unto the Lord. For the husband is the head of the wife as Christ is the head of the church, his body, of which he is the Savior. Now as the husband submits to Christ, so also wives should submit to their husbands in everything. Husbands love your wives, just as Christ loved the church and gave himself up for her to make her holy and blameless. In this same way, husbands ought to love their wives as their own bodies. He who loves his wife loves himself. For this reason a man will leave his father and mother and be united to his wife, and the two will become one flesh.

Colossians 3:19
Husbands love your wives and do not be harsh with them.

Numbers 23:19
God is not a man, that he should lie; nor a son of man, that he should change his mind. Does he speak and then not act? Does he promise and then not fulfill?

Search Yourself!

What fruits of the spirit are operating in my mate's and my life?

_____
_____
_____

What areas of change do I need to pray for in my marriage to be in alignment with what God requires of me and my spouse?

_____
_____
_____

SUBMISSION OR ABUSE

> Submit to one another out of reverence for Christ. Wives, submit to your husbands as to the Lord. For the husband is the head of the wife as Christ is the head of the church, His body, of which He is the Savior. Now as the church submits to Christ, so also wives should submit to their husbands in everything.
> (Ephesians 5:21-24)

"Know the Difference"

It is very important for God's people to be in submission. God wants his people to be in submission to Him, just as Jesus submitted Himself to the Father. Ephesians 5:21 says that believers are to submit to one another in the fear of God. This does not imply in any way that one spouse is to control the other. Many people assume that submission means powerlessness. Webster's 1828 Dictionary describes submission as "the act of yielding to power or authority; surrender of the person and power to the control or government of another". Obedience on the other hand, is described in the same dictionary as "proper submission to authority. That which duty requires, implies dignity of conduct rather than servility".

Making the distinction between submission and control may mean the difference between an anointed marital covenant and the aggravating inconvenience of an abusive relationship. Submission means that you will yield to power. The ultimate power in a believer's life is God. His Word dictates what "proper submission" is. Note that dignity rather than servility is the key. If submission to your spouse violates what your ultimate power, God, requires of you; you must re-evaluate whether your submission is in need of Godly boundaries. These boundaries should not allow for or encourage disobedience to God's word. They should help promote the sinner's [the abuser's] return to righteousness. Maintaining strong boundaries with those who lack self-control is the Godly thing to do.

Seek His Face

Galatians 6:1
Brothers, if someone is caught in sin, you who are spiritual should restore him gently. But watch yourself, or you also may be tempted.

Ephesians 5:33
However, each one of you also must love his wife as he loves himself, and the wife must respect her husband.

Search Yourself?
Are there any areas of submission in my life for which I need to set Godly boundaries? What are they?

_____
_____
_____
_____
_____
_____
_____
_____
_____
_____
_____
_____
_____
_____
_____
_____
_____
_____

UP FRONT AND PERSONAL

> But mark this: There will be terrible times in the last days. People will be lovers of themselves, lovers of money, boastful, proud, abusive, disobedient to their parents, ungrateful, unholy, without love, unforgiving, slanderous, without self control, brutal, not lovers of the good, treacherous, rash, conceited, lovers of pleasure rather than lovers of God- having a form of godliness but denying its power. Have nothing to do with them.
> (2 Timothy 3-5)

"Silhouette of an abuser"

At a distant glance, my abuser seemed like every woman's dream. He was a tall handsome man; 6'4" and approximately 215lbs. He was a truck driver and made good money. He was affectionate and insisted on holding my hand whenever we were out in public. He was helpful, frequently choosing what I should wear. He was concerned and called often to check on me. Sounds like a great husband, right?

WRONG!! Remember that distant glance and all the good things I thought I saw. They were a distortion of what was really there. The packaging was just as I described but inside there was a time bomb waiting to explode. The truck driver who made good money only made good money if he kept a job. He didn't! None of his actions were motivated by love but instead by his need to control me and hinder my growth as a believer and as a woman. His displays of affection were a cover-up, masking his insecurities. He did not choose my clothing because he wanted me to look beautiful. This was his way of controlling the way I dressed and/or an opportunity to demean me for choices that were not his. His frequent calls were necessary for him to be reassured that I was not "up to no good", as he would say. He rarely spoke words of endearment or appreciation. He used drugs on and off for most of his life and most of our marriage. For recreation, he choked, punched, and kicked me. Spitting in my face or on my belongings added a special flare to the abuse. All of these actions were attempts to encourage my continued compliance with the abuse.

If you think my abuser was bad, remember King Saul. Let's look back at the book of 1 Samuel to see another silhouette of an abuser. Remember the relationship of King Saul and David. It demonstrates very clearly what an abuser acts like. Saul exhibited many of the same characteristics. He was insecure, jealous, obsessive, controlling, and had a superiority complex. He often expressed fits of rage. He
frequently made excuses for his behavior or blamed his shortcomings on David, the victim. He stalked David on numerous occasions. He repeatedly physically and emotionally abused David, Jonathan, Michal, and his servants. He manipulated his children and everyone around him in an attempt to enlist their help in carrying out his abuse. He ignored the truth, especially when it validated the abuse. He used his economic status as a license for the abuse.

Sounds extreme? It may be. Some abusers may be more subtle in their chosen forms of abuse. But remember that abuse is abuse and God's word says that abuse is SIN! Sin must be stopped, especially in the life of a believer.

Let's take a closer look at the anatomy of an abuser. Abusers can appear in many forms. They can be any race, gender, body type, rich, or poor. Physical characteristics of a person do not determine who will become an abuser. Despite the wide spectrum of people who perpetrate abuse, some common behavioral characteristics have been
found. Jealousy is often one of the first warning signs of an abusive personality. It may be first confused with love or concern but can quickly become a form of control and coercion. Jealousy may be followed by or accompany fits of rage which serve to intimidate and control the victim.

Psychological abuse, described in Galatians 5:19 as discord and dissensions, even in the absence of physical abuse destroys relationships and homes. Although drunkenness is not the cause of domestic violence, this and misuse of other substances may aggravate or ignite the abuse. It may even provide an excuse for the abuser. Many abusers say that the alcohol or other substances made them "lose control". Also, sexual immorality, impurity, or debauchery may be used as a means of demeaning or causing emotional pain to the victim.
In domestic violence, the abuser wants to dominate and control the victim. Physical violence is usually added to maintain authority. Abusers may use several tactics like physical, sexual, or emotional abuse to control the victim. Verbal or non-verbal threats may also be used. If physical abuse occurs infrequently in your situation, keep in mind that other types of abuse can be just as damaging. The goal of any type of abuse is to instill fear in the victim which allows the abuser to maintain control. Fear give less aggressive forms of abuse like verbal and emotional abuse more damaging power. The abuser often restricts the victim's contact with friends and family to create dependency. Financial resources may be limited or controlled in an attempt to prevent financial independence. This may inhibit the victim's ability to leave the abusive situation. The abuser may criticize or belittle the victim to instill feelings of worthlessness or low self-esteem.
Low self-esteem can trick the victim into feeling like he/she deserved or caused the abuse. Abusers, themselves, often suffer from low self-esteem and their identity may be tied to the role the victim plays in their life. In other words, the abuser may feel validated by his/her ability to maintain control over the victim. By taking control of your life and taking it away from your abuser, the abuser loses power.
 Now that we have a physical and biblical picture of an abuser, let's look at the source of abuse. Although abuse,

especially physical abuse, may seem like a physical war, it is not. Domestic violence is a spiritual war. It is the spiritual weaknesses of the abuser that allows the enemy to operate in his/her life. We, as believers, must recognize that we wrestle not against flesh and blood [the physical being] but against principalities, powers, and rulers of darkness [a spiritual being]. (Ephesians 6:12) We, as believers, must stand against this attack of the enemy on our family. Recognize that we have authority over all the powers of the enemy through Jesus Christ. Know that our weapons of warfare are not carnal but mighty through God to the pulling down of strongholds. (2 Corinthians 10:4) The abuse, if carried out long enough can become a stronghold in the abuser's life that only prayer and faith can break. Domestic violence is a battle of the mind, spirit, and soul. It can be an internal war for the abuser, stemming from abuse he/she may have endured in the past. Unforgiveness towards a past abuser may also act as a catalyst for a person to become a perpetrator of abuse. Domestic violence can also be an emotional war that encompasses many family dynamics. Regardless of the device that the enemy chooses, we must recognize that the real culprit is Satan. His ultimate goal is destruction; of a person, a marital union, or an entire family. 1 Corinthians 7:15 tells us that God calls us to live in peace. How can we live in peace if we allow the enemy to terrorize our households, our spouses, our children, our lives? We must stand on the promises of our Lord and Savior, Jesus Christ, knowing that
He will guide us and protect us if we honor His word. If our abusers are willing to submit to God, they too can be delivered.

Seek His Face

Ephesians 6:12
For we wrestle not against flesh and blood, but against principalities, against powers, against the rulers of the darkness of this world, against spiritual wickedness in high places.

Matthew 5:22
But I tell you that anyone who is angry with his brother will be subject to judgment.

1 Corinthians 7:15
But if the unbeliever leaves, let him do so. A believing man or woman is not bound in such circumstances; God has called us to live in peace.

Psalms 72:4
He shall judge the poor of the people; he shall save the children of the needy, and shall break in pieces the oppressor.

1 Corinthians 5:11
But now I am writing you that you must not associate with anyone who calls himself a brother but is sexually immoral or greedy, an idolater or a slanderer, a drunkard or a swindler. With such a man do not even eat.

1Corinthians 6:9
Do you not know that the wicked will not inherit the kingdom of God? Do not be deceived: Neither the sexually immoral, nor idolaters, nor adulterers nor male prostitutes, nor homosexual offenders, nor thieves, nor the greedy, nor drunkards, nor slanders, nor swindlers will inherit the kingdom of God.

Mark 7:20-23
He went on: "What comes out of a man is what makes him

'unclean.' For from within, out of men's hearts come evil thoughts, sexual immorality, theft, murder, adultery, greed, malice, deceit, lewdness, envy, slander, arrogance, folly. All these evils come from inside and make a man unclean."

Malachi 3:5
"So I will come near to you for judgment. I will be quick to testify against sorcerers, adulterers and perjurers, against those who defraud laborers of their wages, who oppress the widow and the fatherless, and deprive aliens of justice, but do not fear me," says the Lord Almighty.

Leviticus 25:17
Do not take advantage of each other, but fear your God. I am the Lord your God.

Psalms 4:4
In your anger do not sin; when you are on your beds, search your hearts and be silent.

Search Yourself!

What ungodly characteristics do I see in my abuser? How are they expressed?
_____
_____
_____
_____

My prayer for deliverance for my abuser is...
_____
_____
_____
_____

SALT OF THE EARTH

> You are the salt of the earth. But if the salt loses is saltiness, how can it be made salty again? It is no longer good for anything, except to be thrown out and trampled by men.
> (Matthew 5:13)

"Battered"

I was 28 years old when the abuse started. At the time, I was blessed with a beautiful baby girl; the child of my dreams. I was financially stable, working as a nurse in a local hospital. I owned my own home, a car, and had a healthy savings. I enjoyed a fulfilled life surrounded by a great family and wonderful friends. Behind this perfect picture life laid a victim of domestic violence. Sounds unreal? It was, or at least it seemed like it was. It felt like I was having a nightmare from which I could not wake up, but this experience was very real.

So what kind of person becomes a victim? Like we learned about the abuser, anyone can become a victim. Even David, the giant-slayer! Victims can be any age, sex, race, culture, religion, educational level, employment or marital status. Abuse often involves a control of all family dynamics. Many victims become slaves in their homes, having their every move controlled. Abusers may use many tactics to maintain this control. Many times the victim is isolated from family, friends, and community resources. The abuser may call the victim names. Some commonly used names include damaged, crazy, dumb, stupid, ugly, or any one of many other demeaning names. Victims may be told that no one else will want them or that they could never make it on their own. Other victims are told that the abuse is their (the victim's) fault. Some are threatened with harm to themselves, their children, or other loved ones. Occasionally, the abuser may also threaten to take away the children.

David exhibited many of the same behaviors as other victims of abuse. Let's see how his life resembled mine and that of many other victims of abuse. He frequently made attempts to calm his abuser, Saul. My attempts to calm my abuser were to remain silent even if I knew that he was completely wrong; to allow him to have his way at any cost. David blamed himself for the abuse and frequently apologized for his actions. I apologized even when I knew it was not my fault; just to keep peace. David exhibited sympathy for other victims, probably because he knew how they felt. Compassion and empathy are my sole purposes for writing this book. I want to lessen the pain and empower victims. David was loyal to King Saul despite the abuse. David showed concern and offered help to many people and even Saul, his abuser.

Psalms 55 clearly describes how David's abuse made him feel. His emotions mirror the emotions of many victims of abuse. He talks of feeling ignored, troubled, distraught, reviled, and fearful, in agony, horrified, and hated. He felt taunted and betrayed. He describes these feelings as overwhelming. He speaks of wanting to "fly away and find rest". He wants to find shelter "far from the tempest and storm". He describes these feelings as destructive forces at work. In some translations of the Bible, David describes his experience simply as "suffering". I definitely can relate to these feelings. How about you?

Victims of domestic violence try many different tactics to help them to cope, many of them subconsciously. Some victims alter their behavior in an attempt to change the abuser's behavior. Other victims of abuse may try to minimize the seriousness of the abuse in attempts to cope with the situation. Many are ashamed of their situation. Embarrassment can make the victim reluctant to disclose the abuse to loved ones. Many victims end up battling these emotional demons alone.

Abuse, if carried on for long periods of time, can prevent the victim from being able to differentiate reality from lies. Severe or chronic abuse may also cause the victim to have difficulty problem-solving or identifying options. For this reason, it is essential that the victim does not face the abusive situation alone.

"But not Broken"

The closet is the place where we hide things that we do not want anyone to see. It is the place where many abusers and even the victims hide their weakness, misery, pain, or brokenness. For many of us, we believe that if we don't hide our shortcomings that it will allow others to see our weaknesses. Think back to when you have had an unexpected guest and neglected to clean house that day. Where did you put everything you didn't want them to see? In the closet! Let me reassure you that you had the right idea but for the wrong reasons. The closet is the perfect place to put your troubles. That is, if it is a prayer closet.

Despite the many unhappy feelings that domestic violence and abuse evokes in us, God's word provides hope. It tells us that because we have accepted the gift of salvation and have chosen to live in obedience to God's instruction; we are guaranteed certain rewards. Among these are love, happiness, joy, and peace. Domestic violence goes against everything that God has promised us. It not only violates our physical being but our spiritual and emotional wellbeing. Victims of domestic violence need to keep their eyes on the prize, the reward of the high calling of the Lord. Know that the Father wants only the best for you. His Word assures this. Allow the Lord to order your steps in every aspect of your life but especially in ungodly situations. Take yourself out of the equation and allow this awesome God to show you how great He is. Walk in faith knowing that what He promises in His word is already done.

If you are in a relationship that violates these basic biblical principles, several things need to happen to end the abuse. Search yourself for insight into why the abuse is happening. I would often ask myself, 'What is God trying to show me?" What door did I leave open to allow the enemy to move in my life? These questions were not physical in nature. They were my attempts to gain spiritual insight into my situation. They were to evaluate my spiritual walk. Keep in mind that neither you nor I caused our abuse. NO ONE DESERVES TO BE ABUSED! This search serves the purpose of identifying any steps that may have given the enemy, Satan, power in our lives. Remember that there are instances where we can get outside of God's will. This provides the enemy an open door to bring trials and tribulation in our lives. Stand against the enemy who seeks to kill, steal, and destroy all that God has promised you.

Through my spiritual search, I realized several things. My marriage was for a reason and for a season. God used the abuse to create a need in my life that only He could fill. The abuse stimulated a desire in me to find true happiness and inner peace. This desire was quenched with the gift of salvation. God used the turmoil in my life to draw me closer to him. I also recognized that through living in the flesh, I had made some ungodly choices. I realized that I had chosen a mate for myself. God treasures His children. He would not have chosen this mate for me. He has only the best to offer me and YOU!

Once you understand the depth of God's love for you, you will know that one thing is for sure. Our God, the One who is mighty to provide wisdom, refuge, guidance, provision, help, and protection, will bring you out of the abuse and all things will work for your good. You are the salt of the earth and just as salt has to go through the fire to be purified. So will you! But you must know that when you have gone through the fire and been purified by the heat that you will come out stronger, more pure, and more precious.

Seek His Face

Galatians 3:28
There is neither Jew nor Greek, slave nor free, male nor female, for you are all one in Christ Jesus. If you belong to Christ, then you are Abraham's seed, and heirs according to the promise.

Romans 8:28
And we know that all things work together for good to them that love God, to them who are the called according to his purpose

Matthew 7:6
Do not give to dogs what is sacred; do not throw your pearls to pigs. If you do, they may trample them under their feet, and then turn and tear you to pieces.

Search Yourself!

What spiritual doors have I left open in my life that have given the enemy power in my life?
___
___
___

My prayer for deliverance, guidance, and protection is...
___
___
___
___

INVISIBLE TEARS

> Fathers don't aggravate your children or they will become discouraged.
> (Colossians 3:21)

"Children and Abuse"

My daughter was 3 years old the first time she witnessed the abuse. We were out for a family ride. A minor disagreement quickly exploded into a major brawl where I was on the receiving end of numerous punches to my face and body. My precious daughter, whom I had sheltered from so many things, witnessed the entire beating from the backseat of the car. She never said a word. Despite her lack of tears, I knew that she was horrified because I at 28 years old, having had a whole lot of experience under my belt; was in total shock.

Children in an abusive family can be victimized either directly or indirectly. Child abuse, like any other type of abuse can be one dimensional or multi-dimensional. It can be directly perpetrated against the child or the damage can be caused by witnessing the abuse perpetrated upon someone the child loves. It can be physical which consists of shaking, hitting, beating, burning, biting, or any other physical contact that results in injury. Verbal abuse can be emotionally damaging. Demeaning, blaming, or excessive yelling are examples of emotional abuse. Child abuse can be sexual such as fondling, forced sexual activity, or exposure to sexual stimulation inappropriate for the child's age. Child abuse can also be neglectful such as a failure to provide for the child's physical needs i.e. food, clothing, shelter, medical care. Neglect can also include a failure to supply emotional needs such as affection, attention, and supervision.

Children often respond to problems at home with rebellion, disobedience, or mirroring of the same behaviors that the parents exhibit. This disobedience is sin and can, if allowed to continue; push the child away from you and more importantly from the Lord. I did not see the effects that abuse had on my child until years later. My little girl who was raised to know and love the Lord began to act out. She became disrespectful and angry. The loving, affectionate, and compassionate child that I once knew began showing aggression for the simplest things. She was easily agitated. I often found her crying for no reason at all. Her A's and B's in school quickly turned into C's and D's. She began lying about everything. She hid her homework and/or lied about it. She lied to her teachers, her family, and even to herself. This self-assured child, who had an opinion about everything, began to doubt herself, me, and God. She often questioned me about why God was allowing "him" to hurt us. She even went so far as to question God's love for us and his ability to protect us from our abuser.

   The bible tells us that children have a special place in God's heart and harming them is inviting God's wrath. Parents are instructed to be gentle and loving towards their children. Nothing should be done to destroy the spirit of our children or to destroy their innocence. Jesus strongly warns those who cause children to stumble or to lose faith in him that they will be punished. Additionally, the Word tells us that if anyone causes one of these little ones to sin, it would be better for them to have a large millstone hung around their neck and to be drowned in the depths of the ocean. (Luke 17:2) This is not just a warning for the abuser but the victim as well. We must be protectors of our children. We must set Godly examples by not allowing anything that is not of God to operate in our lives. This includes not settling for abuse and more importantly, not allowing it to harm our children in any way.

   Proverbs 22:6 says, "Train a child in the way he should go and when he is old, he will not depart from it."

I believe that there are two sides to this verse. On one hand, God is telling us to raise our children to have Godly values and when they are adults, even if trials come, they will not depart from them. On the other hand, if we set ungodly examples and teach our children to accept ungodly circumstances, they will not depart from these as well. If we don't stop the abuse, we may find our children repeating the same cycle of being abused or perpetrating it on someone else. We must always be conscious of the examples we set for our children, Good and Bad.

"Untouched?"

You might say, but my child has never been physically abused. Neither was mine! Children in abusive homes are being abused even if they are not being physically harmed. Most children who live in abusive environments know about the abuse. Even if there is no physical harm to the child, they can be injured emotionally.

Growing up with abusive parents or in any abusive situation can be a traumatic experience that can affect a child's way of thinking for life. Children exposed to abuse may exhibit pessimism about themselves and their family situation. Some develop low self-esteem. Abuse can hinder their success in school, relationships, or life in general. Some children in abusive families begin to act out by displaying rebellion, anger, frustration, or depression. Others exhibit physical symptoms, such as anxiety attacks and other "unexplained" illnesses, as a manifestation of their emotional pain. Many get involved in sexually inappropriate situations like promiscuity. Abuse of alcohol or drugs can also become a child's way of coping with the abuse. Some children go as far as to run away from home in an attempt to escape the abuse.

Keep in mind that not all children exhibit these behaviors. Some children don't exhibit any external signs of their internal damage. For these children, their tears are invisible. For children who are unable to express how the abuse is affecting them, you should simply know that it is. You must be your children's advocate, their protector, and their strength. You must stand in the gap, interceding on their behalf. You must stop the abuse, even if it means stepping outside of your insecurities. If you don't feel that you have the strength or the resources to do so, allow God to do what He does best; protect and guide those He loves. He will supply all of your needs according to his riches and glory. (Philippians 4:19).

"Through Her Eyes"

As the abuse got worse, so did my daughter's response to it. Her frequent conversation about God and his goodness turned into questions about why God was allowing the abuse to happen. This ultimately was the catalyst for me leaving my situation. It was not until we were delivered from our bondage that my daughter was able to express her feelings to me. Her words pierced the depths of my soul. For a long time, it was the source of much pain for me; knowing that I had not provided the example of strength and Godliness that I had strived to portray. Below, I have described some of her feelings in detail in hopes that it will help you to understand how children see abuse, even those who know and love the Lord.

Her Feelings
Fear - "Will he will kill my mommy?"
- "Will he start abusing me?"
- "Will my mommy get mad at me?"
- "Will my mom take the abuse out on me?"

Sadness - "Seeing my mommy get hurt makes me sad."
- "It makes me want to cry when my mommy cries."

Unloved - "Doesn't anyone care that I am sad?"

Helplessness - "I can't even protect my mommy."

Hopelessness - "He won't ever stop hurting my mommy"
 - "No one cares about us."

Frustration - "Why doesn't God stop him from hurting my mommy?"

Her Guilt
- "It is all my fault."
- "It would not have happened if I had been good."
- "I'm embarrassed."
- "I just don't want to cause any more problems."
- "What will people say about me and my family?"
- "Why couldn't I stop him from hurting my mommy?"

Her Healing

My daughter's healing process was a long process of pain, tears, and fears. My ultimate goal was to eliminate feelings of shame, hurt, and any other lies of the enemy. When I think of her road to recovery, I visualize a stairway to heaven. This is not just any stairway. It is comprised of many small steps up a very long stairwell. Each step was a painful and difficult step toward restoration. Although this path to wholeness was challenging, it was worth it because at the top was the loving, affectionate, compassionate, God-fearing child that I seeked to raise and she was whole again.

Once we were delivered from the abuse, I was able to provide a safe, quiet place where my daughter and I could have long talks. I encouraged her to talk openly and honestly about her feelings. Sometimes she drew pictures to express those thoughts or feelings that she was uncomfortable talking about. We spoke often of our past, but more importantly our plans for the future. We stayed focused on the prize, the joy and blessings of the Lord. I assured her that God had always been and was still in control of our lives and that only He can provide the magnitude of help that we needed. I need her to know that God's word was true and that He would never leave us or forsake us. (Deuteronomy 31:6) We read the Word often and search the scriptures to gain insight into all that God had promised us. I stressed how God had delivered us from our captor and that He would reward us for our diligence and obedience to His Word.

Only after we stepped into the place of authority that God had for us could we begin the spiritual healing. The first step was reassurance in love; my love for her and God's love for us. Open communication was essential for transition from this step. I made sure that she understood that the abuse was wrong. It was SIN!!! I reminded her that no one deserves to be mistreated. I assured her that none of the abuse was her fault. I encouraged her to cry whenever she felt sad. Then we worked on forgiveness. Forgiveness propelled us to the next level by removing the pain and the anger. Then we focused on the importance of obedience to the Word knowing that there was a reward for us if we prevailed. We received many rewards for our obedience and diligence. Among them were joy, peace, and restoration.

Seek His Face

Ephesians 6:4
Fathers do not exasperate your children; instead, bring them up in the training and instruction of the Lord.

Matthew 18:6
But if anyone causes one of these little ones who believe in me to sin, it would be better for him to have a large millstone hung around his neck and to be drowned in the depths of the sea.

Luke 17:1-3
Jesus said to his disciples: "Things that cause people to sin are bound to come, but woe to that person through whom they come. It would be better for him to be thrown into the sea with a millstone tied around his neck than for him to cause one of these little ones to sin. So watch yourselves.

1 Corinthians 10:32
Do not cause anyone to stumble, whether Jews, Greeks or the church of God.

Search Yourself!

Have I seen any negative changes in my child/children that are the result of witnessing the abuse? What are they?
_____
_____
_____
_____
_____
_____

My prayer for my child's restoration is...
_____
_____
_____
_____
_____
_____
_____
_____
_____
_____
_____
_____

HEAVENLY COUNSELOR

> "If your brother sins against you go and show him his fault, just between the two of you. If he listens to you, you have won your brother over. But if he will not listen, take one or two others along, so that 'every matter may be established by the testimony of two or three witness.' If he refuses to listen to them, tell it to the church and if he refuses to listen even to the church, treat him as you would a pagan or tax collector.
> (Mathew 18:15-17)

"By The Book"

In biblical times, pagans were generally defined as those who worshiped false gods. God tells us that people who worshipped false gods would have the wrath of God upon them. (Colossians 3:6) Pagans were viewed with utter contempt probably because they lived in a manner contrary to God's Word. Like pagans, tax collectors were also hated me because they usually operated in extortion and deception. If they, themselves were not dishonest, most were willing to partner with ungodly men. They were viewed as traitors. To eat with a tax collector rendered one spiritually unclean. Tax collectors were both hated and avoided by believers. In the book of Luke, tax collectors were compared to robbers, evildoers, and adulterers. Psalms 37:9 says that they will be "cut off" from the many blessings of the Lord.

Abuse is a serious matter. Believers are responsible for confronting sin. The abuser's soul is at stake and this soul is no less valuable to God. The sin, the abuse, must be stopped. Just like every other expectation that God has for us, He has provided instructions for this task as well. Here is what the instruction manual, the Holy Bible, tells us that we must do. First we must attempt to show our abuser his/her fault. When confronted, many abusers deny the situation and/or escalate the abuse. If this is the case, the scriptures provide evidence that cannot be denied. Pray for insight and revelation into your role in helping your abuser to return to righteousness. If a one on one confrontation is unsuccessful, unrealistic, or it is unsafe for you to confront your abuser alone; you should enlist the help of someone else who can mediate the situation. This can be a godly friend, family member, Christian counselor, or any other trusted confidant who can assist in a safe confrontation of the abuse. If your abuser is still unwilling to stop the abuse, you should tell it to the church. This means to enlist the help of fellow Christians who can intercede and agree in prayer with you, for you and your abuser's deliverance, protection, and ultimate restoration.

Sometimes the abuse or confrontation of the sin is simply too dangerous. When your safety or your life is being jeopardized, confrontation may be an unrealistic expectation. If this is your situation, then your solution is simple. Leave, find a safe haven, and make your attempts at redirection and restoration from a distance.

Seek His Face

Colossians 3:5-6
Put to death, therefore, whatever belongs to your earthly nature: sexual immorality, impurity, lust, evil desires and greed, which is idolatry. Because of these, the wrath of God is coming.

Luke 17:3
So watch yourselves. "If your brother sins, rebuke him, and if he repents, forgive him.

Ephesians 5:11
Have nothing to do with the fruitless deeds of darkness, but rather expose them.

Leviticus 19:17
"Do not hate your brother in your heart. Rebuke your neighbor frankly so you will not share in his guilt."

Matthew 5:44
But I tell you: Love your enemies and pray for those who persecute you.

Luke 6:28
Bless those who curse you, pray for those who mistreat you.

1 John 5:16
If anyone sees his brother commit a sin that does not lead to death, he should pray and God will give him life. I refer to those whose sin does not lead to death. There is a sin that leads to death. I am not saying that he should pray about that.

Psalms 37:9
For evildoers shall be cut off: but those that wait upon the LORD, they shall inherit the earth.

Search Yourself!

Have I omitted any of God's mandates for confronting the sin of abuse in my life? If so, what can I do to help my abuser return to righteousness?

_____
_____
_____
_____
_____
_____

WHAT TO DO UNTIL YOU GET THROUGH

> Therefore put on the full armor of God, so that when the day of evil comes, you may be able to stand your ground and after you have done everything, to stand. (Ephesians 6:13)

"Stand... Knowing that you have done all!"

My abuse started long before I had been restored in the Lord and it did not end once I had accepted the gift of salvation. It actually got worse. Not worse in its physical severity but worse in emotional effects on me and my child. After I received salvation I expected the abuse to just stop. As I grew in my spiritual walk with the Lord, I learned better. In reality, God's word assured me that many trials would come. I quickly learned that by receiving salvation and living in obedience to God that my face and the face of my child was posted on a wanted poster in hell. Satan was seeking to do what he does best; kill, steal, and destroy. I learned that I must STAND on God's Word, STAND on God's promises, and STAND in the gap for my child's soul.

Standing does not mean waiting idly for things to miraculously change. Remember that with prayer and faith, the blood of Jesus will cover us. If you continue to stand on God's Word, this trial will not hinder your spiritual walk. It will propel you into the place that God has for you. Even for a believer, the violence may not stop. The difference must be the change in you and your response to the abuse. I am not by any means implying that the abuse will not hurt just as bad, but with God you can endure. This test is only temporary and out of it will come a testimony that will glorify God.

In my case, I knew that God would not let this experience be in vain. So I stood, knowing that I would persevere;

that God would deliver me, that everything that His Word promised would come to pass. Although abuse changes your ability to love and the level to which you are able to love, God's Word can restore you. Remember the footprints in the sand. God will help you to stand and when you are unable to stand, he will even carry you through.

By the time the abuse had escalated to its worst, both my faith and my obedience to the Lord had grown. I was now a mature Christian, who knew of God's love for me and the authority that I had in the name of Jesus. I learned to recognize Satan and his many devices. Before entering into the many violent incidences that were to follow, I would pray for protection (Psalms 32:7), wisdom (James 1:5), and strength (Isaiah 40:31). I entered into each incident with the goal of glorifying God through my obedience. I armed myself with the garment of praise, thanking Him for blessing me in every aspect of my life, even my marriage. I praised Him in faith for the saved husband that was to come. I fasted often for my husband's return to righteousness, a breakthrough in my situation, and more importantly that I and my child would remain in the will of God. In a domestic violence situation and any other trial in our lives, we must rely on God's Word to provide all we need. We must know that His Word is true.

Seek His Face

Galatians 6:9
Let us not be weary in doing good, for at the proper time we will reap a harvest if we do not give up.

Psalms 32:7
You are my hiding place; you will protect me from trouble and surround me with songs of deliverance. Selah.

James 1:5
If any of you lack wisdom, he should ask God, who gives

generously to all without finding fault, and it will be given to him.

Isaiah 40:31
But they that wait upon the LORD shall renew their strength; they shall mount up with wings as eagles; they shall run, and not be weary; and they shall walk, and not faint.

1 Peter 1:6-7
In this you greatly rejoice, though now for a little while you may have had to suffer grief in all kinds of trials. These have come so that your faith- of greater worth than gold, which perishes even though refined by fire- may be proved genuine and may result in praise, glory and honor when Jesus Christ is revealed.

Search Yourself!

In what areas of my life have I not trusted God to provide everything I need?

_____
_____
_____
_____
_____

A FATHER'S LOVE

"Promises For All Times"

To endure the trials of life, we must rely on the many promises of God. It was the promises of God that brought me through. His Word promises us protection and refuge, especially from false accusations and lies. It promises us provision. He promises to guide us in dark times. He will give us strength when we are afraid. He promises to deliver us from bondage and hurt and protect us from our enemies. He promises to restore us and give us hope for the future. In other words, He promises us every thing we need. You only need to seek His face and you will find Him. (1Chronicles 28:9)

Blessings/Favor
For the Lord God is a sun and shield; the Lord bestows favor and honor; no good thing does he withhold from those whose walk is blameless. Psalms 84:11

Deliverance
The next day John saw Jesus coming toward him and said, "Look, the Lamb of God, who takes away the sin of the world!" John 1:29

Emotional Healing
No lion will be there, nor will any ferocious beast get up on it; they will not be found there. But only the redeemed will walk there, and the ransomed of the Lord will return. They will enter Zion with singing; everlasting joy will crown their heads. Gladness and joy will overtake them and sorrow and sighing will flee away. Isaiah 35:9-10

Fear
So do not fear, for I am with you; do not be dismayed, for I am your God. I will strengthen you and help you; I will uphold you with my righteous right hand. Isaiah 41:10

Guidance
Because he knows the way that I take; when he has tested me, I will come forth as gold. Job 23:10

Guilt
Trust in the Lord with all your heart and lean not on your own understanding; in all you ways acknowledge him and he will make your paths straight. Proverbs 3:5-6

Helplessness
The Lord is my Shepard, I shall not be in want. He makes me lie down in green pastures, He leads me beside still waters, and He restores my soul. He guides me in paths of righteousness for His name's sake. Even though I walk through the valley of the shadow of death, I will fear no evil, for you are with me; your rod and your staff, they comfort me. You prepare a table before me in the presence of my enemies. You anoint my head with oil; my cup overflows. Surely goodness and love will follow me all the days of my life and I will dwell in the house of the Lord forever. Psalms 23

Hope
"For I know the plans I have for you," declares the Lord, "plans to prosper you and not to harm you, plans to give you hope and a future." Jeremiah 29:11

Insight/Revelation
But everything exposed by the light becomes visible, for it is the light that makes everything visible... Ephesians 5:13-14a

Joy
You turned my wailing into dancing; you removed my sackcloth and clothed me with joy. Psalms 30:11-12

Justice
And will not God bring about justice for his chosen ones, who cry out to Him day and night? I tell you, He will see that they get justice, and quickly. However when the son of man comes, will He find faith on the earth. Luke 18:7-8

Physical Healing
And he said unto her, "Daughter, your faith has healed you. Go in peace and be freed from your suffering." Mark 5:34

Re-establishment
In righteousness you will be established: Tyranny will be far from you; you will have nothing to fear. Terror will be far removed; it will not come near you. Isaiah 54:14

Refuge
If you make the Most High your dwelling- even the Lord, who is my refuge- then no harm will befall you, no disaster will come near your tent. He will command His angels concerning you. Psalms 91: 9-11

Rest
"Come to me, all you who are weary and burdened, and I will give you rest." Matthew 11:28

Restoration
I will build you up again and you will be rebuilt, O Virgin Israel. Again you will take up your tambourines and go out to dance with the joyful. Jeremiah 31:4

Spiritual Protection
No weapon forged against you will prevail, and you will refute every tongue that accuses you. Isaiah 54:17

Victory
Who shall separate us from the love of Christ? Shall trouble or hardship or persecution or famine or nakedness or danger or sword? As it is written: "For your sake we face death all day long; we are considered as sheep to be slaughtered." No, in all these things we are more than conquerors through him who loved us. Romans 8:35-37

Wisdom
If any of you lacks wisdom, he should ask God, who gives generously to all without finding fault, and it will be given to him. James 1:5

Search Yourself!

Am I relying on God's promises? If not, in what areas of my life do I need to pray for more faith?

_____
_____
_____
_____
_____
_____
_____
_____

GOD'S WILL NOT OURS

> Trust in the Lord with all your heart, and lean not on your own understanding. In all your ways acknowledge him, and he will direct your paths.
> (Proverbs 3:5-6)

"Repentance and Reconciliation"

Webster's 1828 Dictionary describes reconciliation as the act of reconciling parties at variance; renewal of friendship after disagreement or enmity. It further describes repentance as real penitence; sorrow or deep contrition for sin, as an offense and dishonor to God, a violation of his holy law, and the basest ingratitude towards a Being of infinite benevolence. This is called evangelical repentance, and is accompanied and followed by amendment of life.

Luke 3:8 explains that repentance must be followed by righteous acts. Simply stated, true repentance is recognized by the fruit it produces. Ask yourself, does the abuse, manipulation, and coercion stop? Accountability is an important indicator of true repentance. It allows the abuser to recognize the effects of the abuse and to make a conscious choice to stop it. The Word says that unrepentant abusers will be judged and will not enter the kingdom.

Luke 12:45-46 says that if a servant of God abuses others, he will be punished when Jesus returns and will be treated as an unbeliever. It is important that domestic violence be recognized as sin. The abuser's soul is in peril. A believer should go and prove by the way he/she lives that they have repented.

If reconciliation is to occur, several things must happen. First, we must allow Jesus to be the Lord of our lives. He must rule our households and every aspect of our relationship. If this is not the case and the abuser's will is contrary to this belief, repentance and reconciliation can not occur.

The believer must pray for guidance and be willing to be obedient to God's instructions. Even if separation is necessary to preserve the relationship, the victim should continue to show love and compassion for the abuser. Pray for deliverance from the spirit of abuse. Both the abuser and victim should have individual time with God daily. This will allow their strength to be renewed.

For successful reconciliation, all parties involved must be following the same path. The Word asks, "How can two people be on the same path except if they agree?" (Amos 3:3). They can't! Pray for guidance every step of the way. Share your problems with people who can offer Spirit-lead answers. Seek out resources to help both of you through this process. This may need to be done separately. Reconciliation is only possible if both parties are willing to commit their lives to Christ and make God the head of their household. Find a local Bible-teaching Christian church, and commit yourselves to membership. Additionally, both parties should find spiritually mature Christians who are willing to disciple them and to hold them accountable for their actions.

Sometimes the risk may become too great for reconciliation to be a safe option. When bodily harm, harm to a child, or the risk of death becomes too great, the boundaries must change. It may be necessary to avoid the abuser to ensure safety. Forgiveness and intercession may have to take place at a safe distance. Jesus' formula for confronting sin promotes accountability while providing safety measures for the victim. Matthew 18:15-17 shows that it may be necessary for others to do the confronting. We should not do anything.

Occasionally victims of domestic violence may need to seek protection from their abuser. This may even require a temporary or permanent move to a safe place. The victim may need to separate from the abuser until the abuser receives treatment for the violence. Once a bible-believing Christian counselor to place ourselves or our children in danger.

Occasionally victims of domestic violence may need to seek protection from their abuser. This may even require a temporary or permanent move to a safe place. The victim may need to separate from the abuser until the abuser receives treatment for the violence. Once a bible-believing Christian counselor or spiritual leader has deemed it appropriate for the couple to reunite, they should make every effort to reconcile and live in peace, while continuing counseling.

Change is not always easy, even in the case of true repentance. For reconciliation, both parties must provide a loving environment complete with Godly correction and boundaries. These boundaries should include an intolerance of any type of disobedience including abuse and violence. It may be necessary to get an order of protection to ensure your safety. Whatever the case, you must be willing to forgive your abuser. But keep in mind that forgiveness does not mean reconciliation. Reconciliation should only take place after repentance is evidenced by good fruit (a change in abusive behaviors). Sometimes repeated reiteration of repentance and forgiveness may be necessary for a sinner to be delivered from bondage and to return to righteousness.

Seek His Face

2 Timothy 2:25-26
Those who oppose him he must gently instruct, in the hope that God will grant them repentance leading them to a knowledge of the truth, and that they will come to their senses and escape from the trap of the devil, who has taken them captive to do his will.

Luke 22:42
Father, if you are willing, take this cup from me; yet not my will, but yours be done."

Luke 3:8
Produce fruit in keeping with repentance.

Mathew 7:20
Thus, by their fruit you will recognize them.

Search Yourself!

What fruit have I seen to indicate true repentance in my mate?
_____
_____
_____
_____
_____

Is reconciliation as safe option for me? Why or why not?
_____
_____
_____
_____
_____
_____
_____

WHEN ENOUGH IS TOO MUCH

> For example, by law a married woman is bound to her husband as long as he is alive, but if her husband dies, she is released from the law of marriage. (Romans 7:2)

"When Divorce IS the answer"

My abuse continued for many years. And still, I stood. I stood until God said that I had had enough. For me, enough had come over and over, again. But it wasn't until God said that enough was too much, that I was released from the debt of the abuse. It wasn't until I recognized God's purpose for me and stepped into the place that He had created me for that I received deliverance from my abuser and the grasp of the enemy. On October 17, 2005 I filed for a divorce.

It was as my husband wrapped his hands around my neck with a force strong enough to squeeze life out of me that I was assured that divorce was God's answer for my deliverance. Even though I knew that God had given me the answer to my prayers, the enemy continued to torment me about my decision to divorce my husband. But greater is He that is in me than he that is in the world. God continually used my friends and family to speak into me and confirm what the Lord had revealed to me. While speaking to my friend, Kaye, about my disgust at having "wasted" five years of my life with an abusive spouse; God revealed several things to me through her. Her explanation of why my marriage was not a "waste" helped me to see how God had used the turmoil in my marriage to bring me to a saving knowledge of Him. He used the anguish caused by the abuse, deception, and pain to draw me closer to Him. He will do the same for you. Through her support and Godly insight, I was able to see how God would be glorified through my trials and my deliverance from the abuse. Pray to the Lord and seek His help. Ask the Lord to give you wisdom and guidance. He will direct your path. He will supply all of your needs.

Although it is often difficult to fully apply the scriptures concerning divorce to our lives, we must take comfort in knowing that God understands us and knows our hearts. He will provide the answers for you. God tells us to choose life not death. Sometimes it is necessary to end a relationship in order to preserve life. This may include your natural life but definitely includes our spiritual life. Pray for instruction and guidance for your particular situation. For me, divorce was my answer. Not because my husband was addicted to masturbation and pornography, and not because he was a liar, an adulterer, and an abuser. It was because he was killing the Spirit that lived in me and hindering my love walk with the Lord. God will preserve you for his purpose at any cost, even at the cost of allowing divorce.

Malachi 2:16 says that God hates, divorce but there were several instances where God permitted divorce in the bible. Every circumstance surrounded an instance where violation of a biblical principle allowed someone to be hurt, abused, or violated. For instance, God divorced the northern tribes of Israel in Jeremiah 3 because they violated his commandments. Additionally, Priest Ezra insisted that Israelite men put away their pagan wives and children in Ezra 10. In Deuteronomy, 24 God permitted the Israelites through Moses to divorce their wives because their hearts were hardened toward their wives. Matthew 19:8-9 tells how God permits divorce in the case of marital unfaithfulness. There is debate as to whether this "marital unfaithfulness" extends to just physical adultery or does it include other types of unfaithfulness such as domestic violence, drug abuse, alcoholism, masturbation, pornography, or any other unrepented violation of the marital covenant.

"Diligence or Disobedience"

When does staying married become disobedience? The answer to this question should be simple; when it contradicts the Word of God. My decision to end the abuse, the emotional and spiritual damage to my child, and my constant struggle to find peace in my marriage was out of obedience to God. Little did I know October 17th was the first day of the rest of my life. It was the day that I began to live in the fullness of God's promises. After leaving that courthouse, I was restored to wholeness. It was in being relieved from the bondage of an abusive husband that, the Lord revealed to me the meaning of the words that I spoke of earlier, FREE TO SERVE, FREE TO LOVE, FREE TO LIVE!!! It was at this time that the spirit of heaviness that I had grown so accustomed to wearing was lifted off of me and my purpose revealed.

"Unfaithful?"

So what constitutes marital unfaithfulness? Keep in mind that any disobedience is unfaithfulness. Matthew 5:28 states that anyone who looks at a woman lustfully has already committed adultery with her in his heart. So, does pornography and masturbation constitute marital unfaithfulness? In the Old Testament, Abraham allowed divorce under the instruction of God, because the husbands' hearts had become hardened towards their wives. Does the ability to abuse another human being mean that your heart has become hardened toward that person? Does this hardening of the heart constitute marital unfaithfulness? Unfortunately, I don't have these answers for you. Not because I don't have a very strong opinion about this subject but because only God can answer those questions for you. Only he knows your situation and how things will work for your ultimate good.

"Vowed to Divorce"

Is it divorce or violence that breaks the marriage covenant? Believe me; I am in no way advocating divorce. But in some very volatile situations, the victim may be in jeopardy of losing natural or physical life. 1 Corinthians 7:12-13 validates divorce in the case of a believing spouse married to an unbeliever who wishes to leave the relationship. If the unbelieving spouse does not wish to stay in a marriage with a believer, the believing spouse is released from the marriage vows. Matthew 18:15-17 tells us that a professing Christian who is a chronic abuser might be considered an unbeliever. If a believer decides to continue the abuse, does this imply that he/she wishes to leave the marriage? Only God knows! Each situation will be different. When you struggle with what path you should take, pray to the Father for insight. The Word promises that if you seek Him that He will be found.

"Dead is Dead!"

Romans 6:23 tells us that the wages of sin is death. Romans 7:2 says that a married woman is bound to her husband as long as he is alive, but if her husband dies, she is released from the law of marriage. Unrepentance and chronic abuse will lead to spiritual death. The scriptures tell us this. Is spiritual death what is being referred to in Romans 7? The Word tells us that if the abuser chooses a life of sin, therefore choosing spiritual death, that the believer is no longer bound to the law of marriage.

"For His Glory!!!"

Before making a decision to leave an abusive relationship and especially to seek divorce, you must take your petition to the Lord in prayer. Jesus says to "be still and know that I am." You must wait on God's instructions for your life. Once you have received your answer to leave from God, you must leave in obedience. Walk in faith knowing that God always knows what is best and that He will provide for your every need during your transition.

For some Christians involved in an abusive relationship, divorce may be the answer. Remember that this step must never be taken in the pursuit of any ungodly desires i.e. revenge, fornication, lust, etc. God will not use ungodly means to justify a Godly end. If divorce is your answer, you will be able to see how God will be glorified through it. Psalms 50:14-15 says "Sacrifice thank offerings to God, fulfill your vows to the most high, and call upon me in the day of trouble; I will deliver you and you will honor Me." The act of domestic violence violates everything that God desires for our lives. But evil for evil is never the answer.

Abuse violates everything we know to be right. It can cause even the most devout lovers of God to have ungodly thoughts and actions. Be vigilant in your prayer life and love walk. God expects us to guard our hearts, minds, and bodies from any act of sin, including abuse. Our Heavenly Father will order our steps. We must be obedient in the instructions of the Lord, even when we don't understand the reason for such direction. We must continue to walk in the authority given to us in the name of Jesus, knowing that we have power over all the forces of evil, even our abusers. We must recognize that Satan, our adversary walks about like a roaring lion, seeking whom he may devour.

Seek His Face

Proverbs 3:5-6
Trust in the Lord with all your heart and lean not on your own understanding; in all your ways acknowledge him, and he will make your paths straight.

Ecclesiastes 3:1
There is a time for everything and a season for every activity under heaven.

Mathew 18:8-9
If your hand or your foot causes you to sin, cut it off and throw it away. It is better for you to enter life maimed or crippled than to have two hands or two feet and be thrown into eternal fire. And if your eye causes you to sin, gouge it out and throw it away. It is better for you to enter life with one eye than to have two eyes and be thrown into the fire of hell.

Romans 6:23
For the wages of sin is death, but the gift of God is eternal life in Christ Jesus our Lord

Search Yourself!

Is divorce God's way of delivering me from my abuser? If so, in what ways will this allow me to glorify the Lord?

_____
_____
_____
_____

REFINING THE SALT

> See, I have refined you, though not as silver; I have tested you in the furnace of affliction.
> (Isaiah 48:10)

"Healing the Hurt"

In biblical times, salt was a very precious commodity. It was not only used to purify and preserve foods, it added flavor. It made food enjoyable. You too, are a precious salt that adds your own unique flavor to the world.

Let's look at healing from an abusive situation like salt being refined. There are several steps that must be taken before the salt is able to be used for the purpose that it was created.

In the first step, brine, a sodium saturated solution, is poured into a series of heaters which elevate to temperatures around 300 degrees under high pressure. Just like the brine, victims of domestic violence have to endure the heat for a season. During the salt refining process, the heat and high pressure removes minerals and harmful additives. For victims of domestic violence it may serve the same purpose. God may use the heat and pressure in your life to burn some ungodly things off of you.

For me, my abuse removed pride, anger, strife, contention, and unforgiveness from heart and from my life.

In the second step of the salt refining process the heated brine then goes into a graveler filled with cobblestones to remove the impurities. Think of the act of abuse as the cobblestones. The cobblestones in my life humbled me and gave me compassion for others in similar situations and victims, in general.

The third step includes lowering the pressure so that it can cool the brine and allow crystals to begin to form. I learned that the heat and pressure had a purpose and that it was only temporary, it no longer had a negative effect on my life. I was able to endure with Godly perseverance. I began to understand the magnitude of God's love and how through the abuse He was molding me into a beautiful crystal. No matter how severe the abuse got, I stood in faith for the reward that I knew God had for me. In my case, the crystals of salt that emerged from the heat and pressure of an abusive spouse came forth as a beautiful, whole, and confident woman of God.

In the fourth step, the salt crystals are placed in an evaporator pan and the remaining brine is removed. For me, this step symbolizes my complete assurance in God's promises and my total dependence on him to meet all of my needs.

Lastly, magnetic screens are used to separate the salt into different sizes and the salt is then stored in the appropriate bins. For me this step signifies the separation of those who choose to accept the abuse as a way of life and those who don't. It includes those who are willing to compromise, accepting some level of abuse regardless of what God's Word says. If we know the Lord, then we know that God is love and if He lives in us, then we are love. The anger that exists in an abusive relationship cannot exist in the presence of such love. Because we are the light of the world, the darkness of abuse will be revealed through our diligence to share our stories, our abilities to heal in a Godly fashion, and our willingness to help others to heal. We must stand firm on all that our Lord and Savior has promised us. Abuse is not an option!

Seek His Face

Matthew 3:12
Whose fan is in his hand, and he will thoroughly purge his floor, and gather his wheat into the garner; but he will burn up the chaff with unquenchable fire.

Matthew 5:14
You are the light of the world. A city that is set on a hill cannot be hid.

Job 16:5
But my mouth would encourage you; comfort from my lips would bring you relief.

Jeremiah 17:14
Heal me, O Lord, and I will be healed; save me and I will be saved, for you are the one I praise.

Search Yourself!

What ungodly characteristics have been purged from my life by my abuse?

_____
_____
_____
_____

What areas of my life am I still struggling with?

_____
_____
_____
_____
_____

NO PEARLS FOR THE PIGS

> Do not give to dogs what is sacred; do not throw your pearls to pigs. If you do, they may trample them under their feet, and then turn and tear you to pieces.
> (Matthew 7:6)

"The Treasure Chest"

Matthew 7:6 says that we should not give to unbelievers or the unrepentant what is sacred. Have you given your pearls to pigs? Has abuse altered your ability to love? Have you allowed the abuse to steal any or all of the wonderful things that God has for you? If so, God can restore you. (Joel 2:25) There are many types of jewels in the world, some more precious than others but all with value, whether it is sentimental or monetary. In God's kingdom we are jewels, all unique and precious in our own way. Matthew 13:45 says "Again, the kingdom of heaven is like a merchant looking for fine pearls." We are those fine pearls. We must recognize how valuable we are to understand how detrimental domestic violence is.

There are many treasures that make us who we are. Among them are our morals and values, our emotions, and our actions. These treasures determine the type of jewel we will become. God's anointing then gives our jewels value. As believers, we have been bought with a price, the blood of Jesus. We must recognize how precious this makes us. God has a plan and purpose for our lives and the lives that we have been given charge over, our children. Abuse violates and devalues our treasures. It hinders our ability to illuminate the world as jewels do.

Know that you are sacred, as sacred as cultured pearls. Protect your precious pearls by setting healthy boundaries for your life. Identify the significance of your purpose here on earth and in the kingdom of God. Never lose sight of how precious of a jewel you are. Understanding the difference between submission and godly boundaries will help you to do this. If you have been devalued or lost your ability to illuminate the world because of abuse, know that God can restore your value. Look to him for guidance on what you need to do to be restored. Then be obedient to God's instructions for your life.

Seek His Face

Joel 2:25
And I will restore to you the years that the locust hath eaten, the cankerworm, and the caterpillar, and the palmerworm, my great army which I sent among you. (NKJV)

Proverbs 3:15
She is more precious than rubies; nothing you desire can compare with her.

Proverbs 31:10
Who can find a virtuous woman? for her price is far above rubies.

Search Yourself!

What treasures make me a precious jewel?

_____
_____
_____
_____

What precious treasures has my abuser stolen or damaged? How can they be restored?

_____
_____
_____

SOUP FOR YOUR SOUL

> Be kind and compassionate to one another, forgiving each other, just as in Christ, God forgave you.
> (Ephesians 4:32)

Just as chicken soup soothes us when we don't feel well. Putting these ingredients in soup for your soul will help you to move past the abuse, separation, divorce, and any other thing that the enemy uses to attack you.

HOLY SOUL SOUP

Ingredients:
- Forgive God!
- Forgive Yourself!
- Forgive Your Abuser!
- Prayer
- Faith

1. Mix complete forgiveness in a man or woman of God.
2. Stir in a healthy portion of daily prayer.
3. Add just a mustard seed of faith.

Note: Fasting should be added for additional flavor.

Serving Size: Unlimited portions

Seems simple? It really is, once you make up your mind to live entirely for God. Complete healing from domestic violence and abuse requires that all unforgiveness, hatred, hurt, and anger be removed from your life. Removing these hindrances allows your relationship with the Lord to flourish, your love for yourself to increase, and your feelings for your abuser to be a catalyst for growth instead of an obstacle.

If you find this hard to do, you only need to look at the greatest example of forgiveness ever set. Jesus lived forgiveness daily but his greatest example was set on the day he was crucified. He came to earth, lived without sin, and chose to bare our sins on the cross. He was tortured and murdered so that we could be free; free from bondage, abuse, sin, and death. During His walk of life to the cross he experienced betrayal, false accusations, injustice, and physical and verbal abuse. Yet, before He died on the cross, he said, "Father forgive them for they do not know what they are doing" (Luke 23:34). Luke 17:3-4 encourages us to forgive those who sin against us, if he/she repents and asks for forgiveness. According to Webster's 1828 Dictionary, forgiveness means, " The act of forgiving; the pardon of an offender, by which he is considered and treated as not guilty. The forgiveness of enemies is a Christian duty." Forgiveness is not only the first but one of the greatest steps that you will take in your recovery. Through forgiveness of God, yourselves, and your abusers, you can be restored.

Satan wants to utilize unforgiveness to create strongholds in our lives. We must recognize that there is a high price to unforgiveness but an even greater reward for forgiveness. Unforgiveness will not protect us nor will it prevent us from being abused again. To the contrary, it will hinder our
walk with the Lord and ultimately deteriorate our faith and spiritual growth. Regardless of whom your anger or

feelings of betrayal targets, forgiveness is the only way that you can completely heal.

Forgiveness is an action not a feeling. You can choose to release bitterness, anger, and resentment even if you don't "feel" like doing so. Forgiveness requires faith which is necessary for us to operate in the fullness of God. Forgiveness promotes spiritual growth especially if your anger is toward God. It allows you to see God's purpose for your trial. Forgiveness not only frees you up to love your abuser but it allows you to love yourself again.

SINLESS

> For I know the plans I have for you," declares the LORD, "plans to prosper you and not to **harm** you, plans to give you hope and a future.
> Jeremiah 29:11

"Forgiving God"

Sometimes the hurt of life's experiences causes us to question God's love for us. We may experience feelings of anger or disappointment. Sometimes we even lose the ability to trust God. Many of us have wondered why God allows bad things to happen to good people. Don't think that you are alone.

Several men and women in the bible have experienced the same feelings of anger, distrust, frustration, or desertion. In John 11, when Lazarus died, his sisters Martha and Mary struggled with disappointment in God. Moses became frustrated with God during the continued disobedience of the Israelites in Numbers 11. In Mark 4, the disciples questioned God's ability to protect them during the storm. David frequently expressed concern that God had forgotten him. Even Jesus questioned God about why he had forsaken him. In all of these circumstances, one fact remained true. They all had to forgive God to be able to see His purpose for their trial.

When we think that God has forgotten us we must turn to God's promises for reassurance. Remember that He is not a man that He should lie. God will do what His word says He will do. Recognize that God has not forgotten us through our trial. Instead, abuse and any other trial is the work of an evil being, Satan, whom we have allowed to distort the truth. This evil must be rebuked. We must do battle! One of our greatest weapons is to forgive the one whom we think has caused harm to come to us, even if it is God.

Jesus tells us in John 16:33 that we will experience troubles in this world. Some will be the result of our own bad choices.

We must recognize our anger toward God and ask for His forgiveness, His guidance and His protection. We must make our concerns known to Him. Remember that his word says that he will never leave you nor forsake you (Hebrew 3:15; Matthew 28:20) Remember that all things will work for the good of those who love the Lord and are called according to his purpose. (Romans 8:28) God will redeem your hurt and heal you. (Isaiah 53 & 64) He will turn your tragedy into triumph for his glory. He will heal those around us, even our abusers. (2 Corinthians 1:4) The abuse is only training ground for our ultimate purpose, to rule and reign with God forever. (Revelation 20:6)

Remember that you do not have to go through this trial alone. God has placed angels around you who can stand in the gap for you. Seek out intercessors that can agree with you and/or pray for you. (Ephesians 3:14-21) Forgiving God allows us to grow stronger and closer to Him. Allow Him to prove Himself faithful to you. (2 Thessalonians 3:3) He will!!!

Search Yourself!

Is there unforgiveness in my heart towards God? What specific areas of unforgiveness am I harboring?
_____
_____

What has God done in my life to prove himself faithful to me?
_____
_____

HIGHLY ESTEEMED

> There is therefore now no condemnation for those who are in Christ Jesus. (Romans 8:1)

"Forgiving Yourself"

Sometimes the hardest person to forgive is ourselves. This was my greatest struggle. I found it difficult to forgive myself for not stopping the abuse but more importantly for the damage it did to my daughter. It saddened me to think about how my bad choices had affected her and might affect her ability to live the blessed and righteous life that God had promised her. Would she look for the same type of man to be her husband? Would she end up in an abusive situation? If so, did I equip her with enough knowledge of the heavenly Father's plan for her life that she would be able to make the right decision regarding her situation? It brought me to tears to see my child lose sight of how awesome God is. She began to doubt me when I would say that God would bring us out of this situation and that He would strengthen us. That look of emptiness was almost more than I could bear. At one point, the changes in my daughter seemed almost unforgivable.

As I grew closer to the Lord, learned His Word, and developed a personal intimacy with Him, I was able to stand firmly on my faith in God and His promises. The Holy Spirit reminded me that guilt was a device of the accuser, Satan. I knew that there were intercessors praying for me and my child. I stood covered in the blood of Jesus knowing that it would take away my sin, the guilt, and the unforgiveness. Since I knew that praise was a necessary weapon in any spiritual battle, I started praising God daily for deliverance from the bondage, forgiveness of my sins, and protection and guidance for me and my child. One day, I don't think I even know when it happened; but the feeling of guilt was taken from me. I was able to forgive myself the forgiveness that was mine all along.

Search Yourself!

Is there something in my domestic violence situation for which I blame myself? Who is really at fault?

_____
_____
_____
_____

POURING OUT POISON

> So watch yourselves. "If you brother sins, rebuke him, and if he repents, forgive him. If he sins against you seven times in a day and seven times comes back to you and says, I repent, forgive him.
> (Luke 17:3-4)

Forgiving Your Abuser

We need to pray for our abusers and allow God to be the judge of them. This does not mean praying for and/or expecting bad things to happen to our abuser. It means that we should forgive our abusers. We must pray for their souls, petition the Lord for their deliverance from their ungodly ways and ask the Holy Spirit to move in their lives. We must be still and know that He is God.

Remember, Satan is the real enemy. Our God has given us authority over all the powers or darkness, even Satan. Praying for those who have harmed you can offer freedom and restoration. Luke 6:28 tells us to bless those who curse us and pray for those who mistreat us. Our abusers need our prayers as God's wrath and Satan's grasp is upon them.

Search Yourself!

Have I forgiven my abuser? If not, what areas of healing must I focus my prayer on in order to forgive him/her?

_____
_____
_____
_____

Seek His Face

Romans 12: 17
Do not repay evil for evil. Be careful to do what is right in the eyes of everybody.

Ephesians 6:12
For our struggle is not against flesh and blood, but against the rulers, against the authorities, against the powers of this dark world and against the spiritual forces of evil in heavenly realms. 2

Thessalonians 3:3
But the Lord is faithful, and He will strengthen and protect you from the evil one.

Romans 12:19
Do not take revenge, my friends, but leave room for God's wrath, for it is written: "It is mine to avenge, I will repay," says the Lord.

Mark 11:25-26
And when you stand praying, if you hold anything against anyone, forgive him, so that your Father in heaven may forgive your sins.

Matthew 6:14-15
For if you forgive men when they sin against you, your heavenly Father will also forgive you. But if you do not forgive men their sins, your Father will not forgive your sins.

Matthew 18:21-22
Then Peter came to Jesus and asked, "Lord, how many times shall I forgive my brother when he sins against me? Up to seven times?" Jesus answered, "I tell you, not seven times, but seventy-seven times."

Luke 6:28
Bless them that curse you and pray for them that despitefully use you.

Acts 26:16-18
Now get up and stand on your feet. I have appeared to you to appoint you as a servant and as a witness of what you have seen of me and what I will show you. I will rescue you from your own people and from the Gentiles. I am sending you to them to open their eyes and turn them from darkness to light and from the power of Satan to God, so that they may receive forgiveness of sins and a place among those who are sanctified by faith in me.

THE POWER OF PRAYER

> The Lord is nigh unto all them that call upon him, to all that call upon him in truth.
> (Psalms 145:18)

"Intimate Petitions"

Prayer is laying down all claims to power and yielding to God for his will to be done. It invites God's power in and breaks the enemy's hold over our lives. Prayer will keep us from entering into temptation. It allows God to transform us, those around us, and/or our circumstances. Prayer humbles us. Prayer establishes a hedge of protection around us and our loved ones.

The Word tells us that we must pray with ceasing. (1 Thessalonians 5:17). Philippians 4:6 tells us that we should give thanks in everything and make our needs known to God. Our prayers must be detailed and fervent. (James 5:16). John 16:24 and Matthew 21:22 tells us that if we ask, that we will receive. Matthew 18:18 says that "whatever you bind on earth will be bound in heaven, and whatever you loose on earth will be loosed in heaven. Jesus gives us the authority in Jesus name to stop evil and permit good. Prayer is the method for achieving this spiritual victory. The Word tells us that believers are to pray for those who mistreat them. Abusers are trapped in a cycle of sin which may be spiraling out of control. The abuser who seems to have all the control ultimately may be the most out of control. Jesus tells us in John 16:23 that whatever we ask in the Father's name will be given to us. This includes deliverance from the bondage of abuse, deliverance of our abusers from the grip of an abusive spirit, protection for our families and ourselves, reconciliation, restoration, and salvation; to say the least. On the following page is a prayer that I have prayed many times, either in part or whole. Try to commit it to memory. As I quickly learned and you might know as well, abuse does not always permit time for a search of the scriptures. You must be armed for battle at all times by having the Word sown in your heart.

RESTORATION PROCLAMATION

Lord, bring my abuser to repentance and a knowledge of the Your truth. Help (name) to see that abuse is a trap of the devil and that he/she is being held captive. Help my abuser to realize that abuse is sin. Open (name's eyes so that he/she can see the light, even in his/her darkness. Forgive (name) for his/her sins and restore him/her to wholeness.

Lord, help me to heal completely from the hurt so that I can be all that you have called me to be. Cleanse me of anything that is not of You. Give me a heart to work in love,
peace, and joy. I confess any times that I've been unloving, angry, resentful, disrespectful, or unforgiving and I ask for forgiveness right now. Restore me to wholeness. Grow me into a confident man/woman with a strong mind, soul, and
spirit. Make me a new person with a Godly prospective so that I can be used for Your glory.

In Jesus Name...Amen

Seek His Face

James 5:16
Therefore confess your sins to each other and pray for each other so that you may be healed. The prayer of a righteous man is powerful and effective.

1Thessalonians 5:17
Pray without ceasing.

Isaiah 30:19
O people of Zion, who live in Jerusalem, you will weep no more. How gracious he will be when you cry for help! As soon as he hears, he will answer you.

Romans 12:12
Be joyful in hope, patient in affliction, and faithful in prayer.

Philippians 4:6
Do not be anxious about anything, but in everything, by prayer and petition, with thanksgiving, present your request to God.

Matthew 21:22
If you believe, you will receive whatever you ask in prayer.

2 Chronicles 7:14
My people, who are called by my name, will humble themselves and pray and seek my face and turn from their wicked ways, then will I hear from heaven and will forgive their sin and will heal their land.

Matthew 26:41
"Watch and pray so that you will not fall into temptation. The spirit is willing, but the flesh is weak."

Search Yourself!

Have I been maintaining a prayer life that is pleasing to God? What do I need to change to cover everyone I love in prayer?

_____
_____
_____
_____

SPIRITUAL SWAP-MEET

> Yet when they were ill, I put on sackcloth and humbled myself with fasting.
> (Psalms 35:13)

"Fasting for a Breakthrough"

Fasting is more than just a denial of the body to having food. Fasting is abstaining from food for a spiritual reason. It is a spiritual affliction of the body. It is denying our flesh to allow spiritual breakthroughs to occur. It has been used for hundreds of years and for many different breakthroughs. Daniel, Moses, David, Nehemiah, Esther, and Jesus among many other people and groups, all fasted. It allows for clear communication with the Father and strengthens our relationship with Him. Fasting always occurs together with prayer. It adds power to your prayers. You can pray without fasting but you can't fast without prayer.

Fasting serves many purposes. It is used to petition the Lord on your behalf or on behalf of someone else i.e. the abuser or our children. In 2 Samuel 12:22, fasting was used to petition the Lord in an extreme situation. It was a means of healing during times of mourning. (1 Kings 21:27) It was used to give praise to God. (Acts 13:2) Ezra proclaimed a fast to incite humility in his people. (Ezra 8:21) Fasting provides supernatural provision for your needs. One major function of fasting is as a tremendous weapon during spiritual warfare. It can offer deliverance from bad habits, even abuse. Fasting increases your spiritual perception by removing distractions from your life to make
God's revelations clear.

There are several types of fasting described in the bible. Allow the Holy Spirit to lead you to the type of fast that is appropriate for you and your situation. Make sure that you commit yourself to the type of fast that you can complete.

Fasting can be done singly or in a group. It can be a partial fast which entails giving up one type of food or other substance. Some people choose to sacrifice a certain food or meal, such as breakfast, lunch, or dinner. Others may drink only water or juices. It can be a total fast which is the denial of all oral intake for a set period of time. Fasting says to God that food and our desires are secondary to His will.

Seek His Face

Isaiah 58:6
Is not this the kind of fasting I have chosen: to loose the chains of injustice and untie the cords of the yoke, to set the oppressed free and break every yoke?

Daniel 9:3
So I turned to the Lord God and pleaded with him in prayer and petition in fasting, and in sackcloth and ashes.

2 Samuel 12:22
He answered, "While the child is still alive, I fasted and wept. I thought, "Who knows? The Lord may be gracious to me and let the child live."

Acts 13:2
While they were worshiping the Lord and fasting, the Holy Spirit said, "Set apart for me Barnabas and Saul for the work to which I have called them."

Ezra 8:21
Then I proclaimed a fast there, at the river of Ahava, that we might afflict ourselves before our God, to seek of him a right way for us, and for our little ones, and for all our substance.

Search Yourself!

Do I have any areas of my life for which fasting can provide a breakthrough? They are...

_____
_____
_____
_____
_____
_____
_____

Fasting Creed

Father God,

I am fasting for _____.

I will abstain from (food/meal)_____
for (length of time)_____.

I will focus my bible study on
(scripture/topics)
_____
_____
_____
_____

_____

In Jesus' Name, Amen

BREAKTHROUGH NOTES:
_____
_____
_____
_____
_____
_____
_____
_____
_____
_____
_____

VICTORY IN JESUS

> The Lord is a refuge for the oppressed, a stronghold in times of trouble. Those who know Your name will trust in You, for You, Lord, have never forsaken those who seek You.
> (Psalm 9:9-10)

"Life after abuse, separation, and divorce"

For complete healing to occur, we must draw nigh to the Lord. We must be obedient to His Word. He is the strength that will lead us out of our bondage and into the light that will brighten our path to the new life that he has for us. For me, life is greater than I ever thought it could be. I have been blessed with the gift of salvation and to be a part of an awesome bible-believing church. I have developed an intimate relationship with my heavenly Father, who has strengthened me beyond belief. I have been reunited with my high school sweetheart, who is a
wonderful man of God. I have grown as a woman, as a mother, and as a believer. I give God all the glory for my deliverance, for my joy, and most importantly for my life.

Seek His Face

Hebrews 13:5
Keep your lives free from the love of money and be content with what you have, because God has said, "Never will I leave you; never will I forsake you."

Proverbs 27:12
The prudent see danger and take refuge, but the simple keep going and suffer for it.

Search Yourself!
What spiritual blessings have I received from my obedience to God's plan for my life?

_____
_____
_____
_____
_____
_____
_____

HELP FOR THE HELPMATE

> Give thanks to the Lord, call on his name; make known among the nations what he has done. Sing to him, sing praise to him; tell of all his wonderful acts. Glory in his holy name; let the hearts of those who seek the Lord rejoice. Look to the Lord and his strength; seek his face always.
> (Psalms 105:1-4)

"The Gift"

Remember the awesome King who rescued me from the abusive prince who turned into a frog. He can do the same for you. He wants to shower you with many gifts. Among the many gifts is the gift of salvation and other spiritual gifts that He has saved up just for you. All you have to do is use your claim ticket. I have included it in this book for your deliverance and redemption through Jesus Christ.

CLAIM TICKET

For: YOU!!
Expiration Date: Never
Best Time to Use: Now

Father God, today I confess to you that I am a sinner. I believe that your son, Jesus Christ, died for my sins and was raised for my restoration. I receive and confess him as my personal Savior right now. I ask you to come into my heart and change me for your glory.

In Jesus Name...Amen

HEALING THE HURT
(Resources For Victims & Perpetrators of Abuse)

Emergency Help
Call 9-1-1

National Domestic Violence Hotline
(800) 799-SAFE
(800) 787-3224

National Council on Child Abuse and Family Violence
(800) 222-2000

National Coalition Against Domestic Violence
1120 Lincoln Street, Suite 1603
Denver, CO 80203
Email: mainoffice@ncadv.org
1-800-799-7233 (hotline)
(303) 839-1852

National Center for Victims of Crime
Monday-Friday 8:30 a.m. - 8:30 p.m.
1-800-211-7996
E-mail: gethelp@ncvc.org

National Organization for Victim Assistance
24 hours a day, 7 days a week
510 King Street, Suite 424
Alexandria, VA 22314
703-535-NOVA (general information)
1-800-879-6682 (referrals)

www.ingramcontent.com/pod-product-compliance
Lightning Source LLC
Chambersburg PA
CBHW071737040426
42446CB00012B/2386